Poetry

Comics

from

THE BOOK OF

Hours

POETRY COMICS

FROM THE

BOOK OF HOURS

BIANCA STONE

PLEIADES PRESS

ISBN: 978-0-8071-6370-2

Published by Pleiades Press

Department of English
University of Central Missouri
Warrensbsurg, Missouri 64093

Distributed by Louisiana State University Press

Cover art by Bianca Stone
Book design by David Wojciechowski
Author's photo by Hillery Stone

First Pleiades Printing, 2016

Financial Assistance for this project has been provided by the Missouri Arts Council,
a state agency, and the National Endowment for the Arts.

CONTENTS

for Matthew Rohrer

who first said POETRY COMICS *to me*

This is a microscopic caress at a party that burns until 5am.

this is the dead fathoming

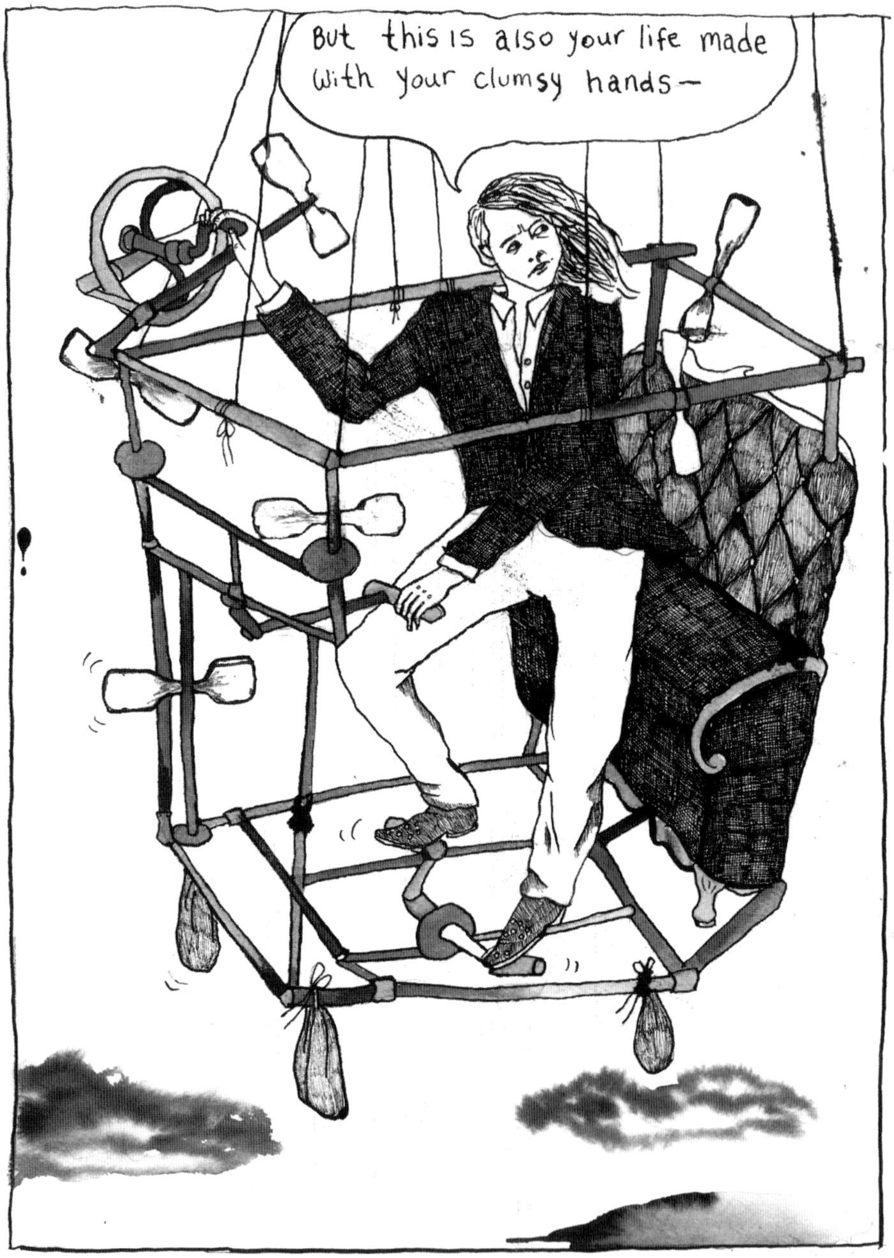
But this is also your life made with your clumsy hands—

Your brain lighting up

When you see a beautiful woman
eating French fries in a dark bar.

Your head split down the middle
by a brook; each hemisphere
divine, witchy —

Out of your depths—your trouble. Your grief speaking.
And your heavy body is getting up and going.
The crazy, absent fathers, all breaking wind in a fire—
the fire engorged.

The dead;

They are still listening.

They want to be loved.

They want

to be remembered correctly.

This is leaving a dark bar with them.

In the cab ride home you lay in each others arms.

~~Talking To a Higher Power~~
~~or~~

Because I Love You I Can Come Apart

                 a jjj

hello this is your car speaking. This is your lover
speaking. ~~Let all the Matthews in the world come forth.~~

    this is your mother speaking. come home and bring me
ten rolls of toilet paper and cigarettes and your gorilla heart.
~~This is your steamboat~~ *speaking* that lies drunk on the warf
and thatsound you hear is the picnic bench
weathering in the wind
                    speaking
but this is also your handmade life, your
desese of the brain
that lights up half a city   that blooms through winter
in an ice machine.   what i wanted to tell you was that
my head is split with a brook. And each he mesphere
is a soft beach, alone with a single drowned god .

My love ~~wherexxxthexexarexdxxxxx~~   out of the depths i
~~conjured the grandmother. And~~ how ~~xxixx~~ sharp her
voice was through the laundry of dark. How many fabulous
organic creams she rubbed on her skin-- and we were there
in the thicket of woods and winter sun, our little
sighing crotches , we stood in the wind long enough to
know it was empty ~~of anything~~. We held onions in our hands,
to our mouths.   Hello this is your

trouble, your grief, your cartoon. This is your midnight dream
of the summer. this is your heavy body1 this is your grusome
~~pertraitxefx~~ bravery. this is your head hurting. this is your
brother crying violet moths and digital advancements. Th is is
the edge of the world where the dead live out their lives
on beautiful houseboats x, late into the night
with their wind-up radios playing soft jazz and birdsongs.
This is the crazy absent father farting into the fire.
This is the fire that has never gone out, and the earth
~~thatxisxrichxxinxme~~ as seen through the eyes of a snowglobe,
and the earth covered in a happy ~~spring~~ glow
and the ~~xxxrth~~ earth filled with the daed who decompose
naturally in the mountains in a vortex of quilts and roots.
~~Butxwherexdexthexex~~ And they all want to be loved . and liked.
these goddamn children. and they all want to be given
things and brought to the river
and fed coffee and blasts of warm ~~warmxx~~ air.
but i am only a ~~x~~ small, fistfull of mint.
~~AndxIxamx~~I am ~~dust~~ bone-dust. I am reading the Collected Stories
of Lydia Davis and ~~my~~ buckeling. I am inventing
a clear cold ghost.~~xIxamxcarryingxaxtinyx~~i whose optic nerve
reflectes our true sentiments. Loyalty, it said slowly
into ~~xx~~ my ear, there has never been any question.

            V
          of that

for
my ladies,
whose beauty
& sorrow
are great.

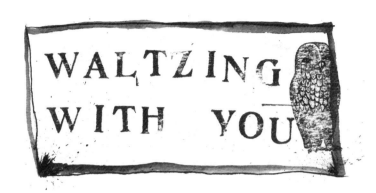

I WANT TO OPEN
THE MOUTH GOD GAVE YOU,

BEAUTIFUL MUTANT.

I FEEL SENTIMENTAL

WHEN YOU SIT DOWN
AT YOUR DESK
PLAYING YOUR LIVE-FEED
VIDEO GAME

YOU'RE REALLY
DOING A WALTZ.

AND SMOKE A CIGARETTE
OVER YOUR SHOULDER...

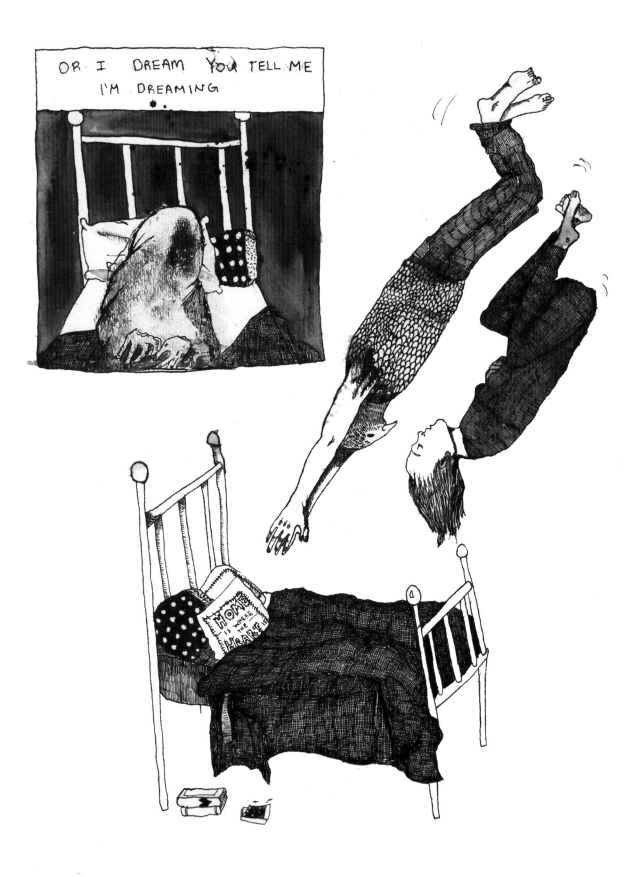

AND I FEEL

A LITTLE BETTER.

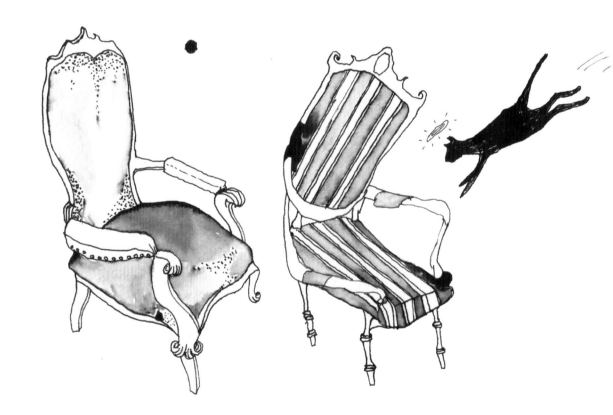

LES MISÉRABLES
THE POEM

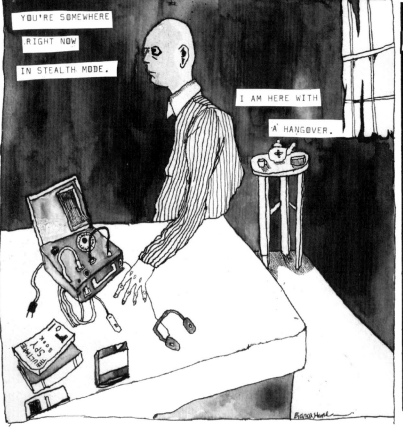

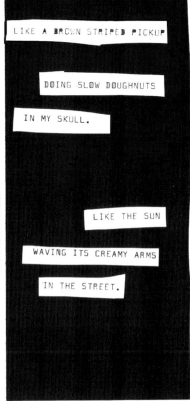

BUT I LOVE THE WORD miserables.

IT ROUNDS OUT IN MY MOUTH

UNTIL MY WHOLE MOUTH

IS WARM.

A HUNDRED BEAUTIFUL BOXES OF GEODES

COULDN'T MAKE ME HAPPIER;

SHIPS OF WET

GUNPOWDER.

COULDN'T MAKE ME

ME HAPPIER.

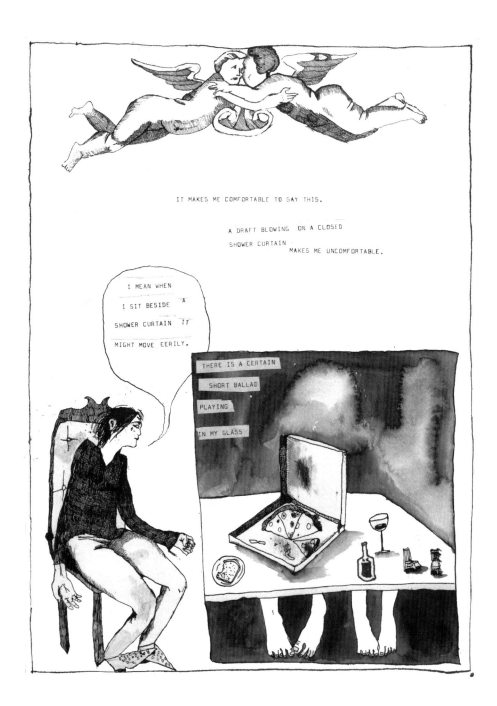

IT MAKES ME COMFORTABLE TO SAY THIS.

A DRAFT BLOWING ON A CLOSED
SHOWER CURTAIN
                MAKES ME UNCOMFORTABLE.

I MEAN WHEN
I SIT BESIDE A
SHOWER CURTAIN IT
MIGHT MOVE EERILY.

THERE IS A CERTAIN

SHORT BALLAD

PLAYING

IN MY GLASS

WHEN I WAS AFRAID I SPOKE TO MY BROTHER ABOUT MY SKILL
WITH KNIVES

    AND WE SAT UP ALL NIGHT BACK TO BACK, SINGING.

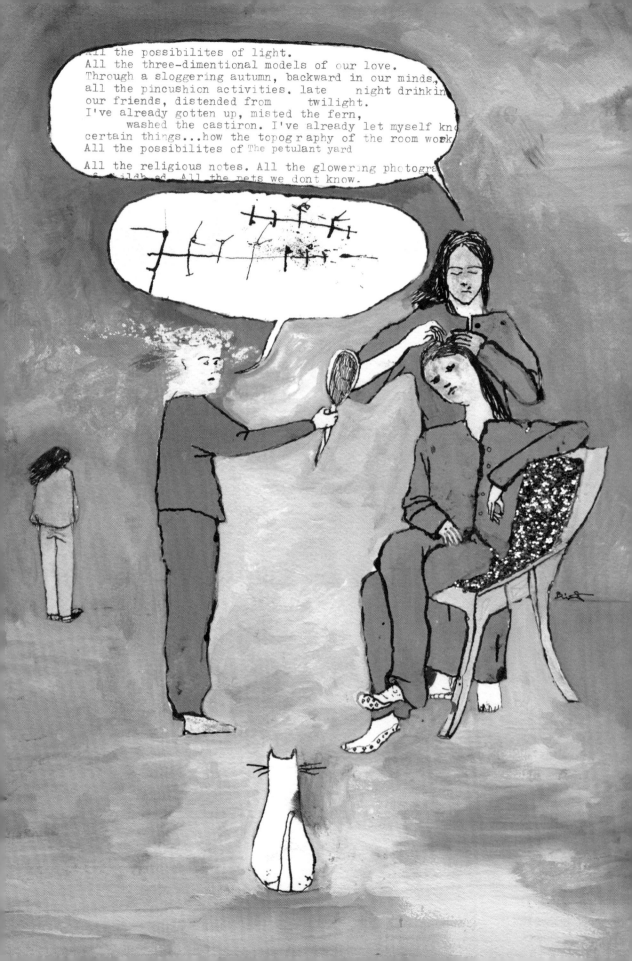

TODAY I WOKE UP BAFFLED.

We Dust the Walls

A Poetry Comic by Bianca Stone

Now we can begin.

In the boudoir, in the hall, back to the ocean that tastes like an old-fashioned—

Bittersweet, the grey-faced world
more than half-hidden by it
and above,
the black, twisted stars—

Out in the pine grove
In the hut my
Uncle built
My father's baby grand
rotting away.

Under its hood
raccoons and mice have
made a   bed
of   Insulation and
Wallpaper; the front door
fell off.

The hut sits—wetbrained, old gypsy,
Waiting with only its mute piano
and piano shawl
of dust.

I keep standing on deck—
Pointing towards the cliffs—

Leave it to me— I'll rule this group of stories— I think I will be ruthless.

Back then
I was
all-in.
I pulled through
like an
upholstery
needle...

My study is wired
with delicate, Scholarly
Explosives.

There is occasional
Singing from the
Pitch-perfect Void.

...one who cannot leave the prison of pleasure and Life!
BIANCA STONE

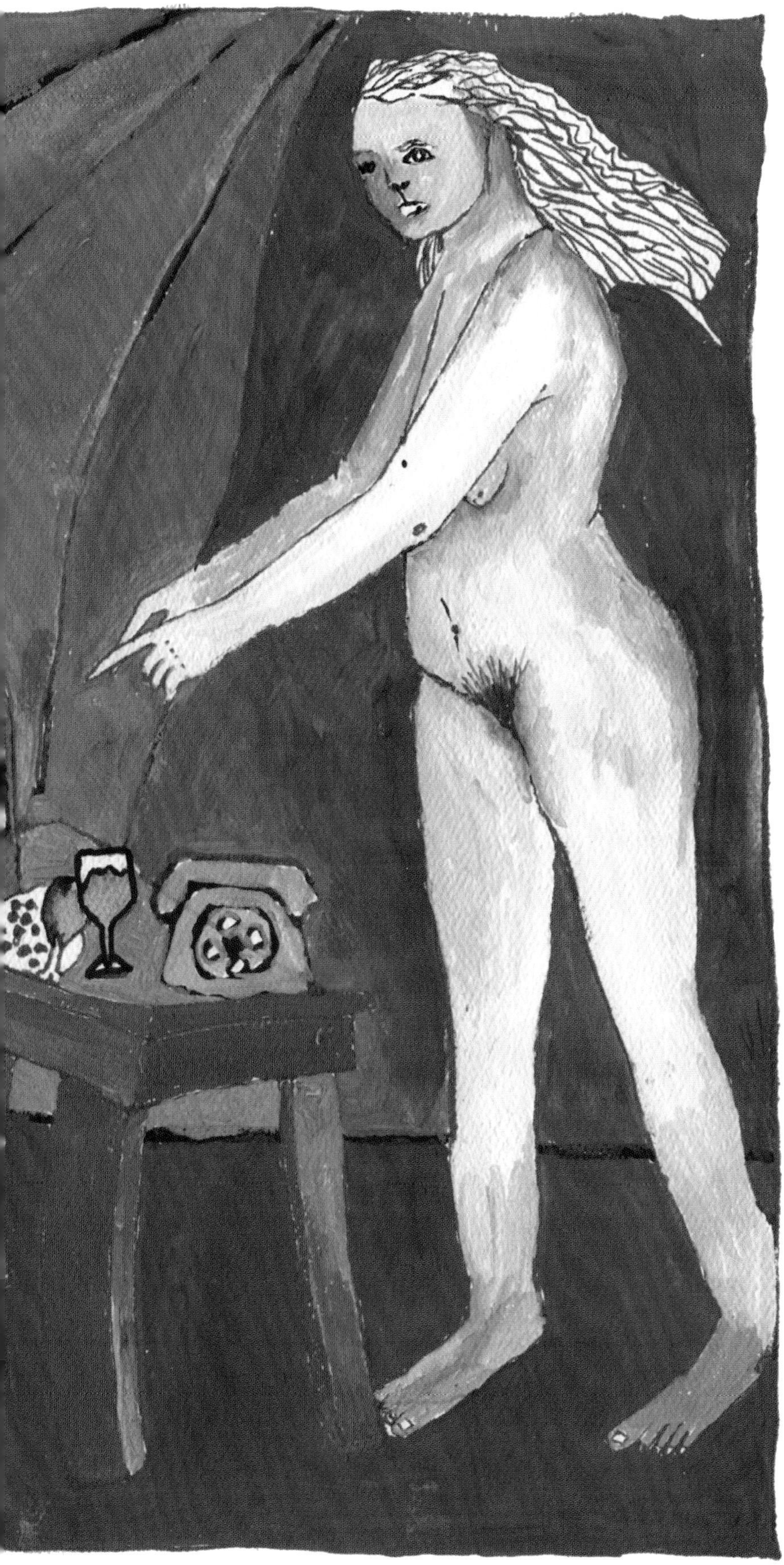

The artist would like to thank Emily Pettit and Factory Hollow Press for publishing "I Want To Open The Mouth God Gave You, Beautiful Mutant," and "Because You Love You Come Apart" in limited edition chapbooks. And the artist would also like the magazines where these poetry comics first appeared:

"Because You Love You Come Apart" [selections], *Nashville Review*

"We Dust the Walls," *The Georgia Review*

"How It Is," *Brooklyn Rail*

"Before Long," *The California Journal of Poetics*

"Noon," *Poetry*

The artist would also like to thank Kathryn Nuernberger and David Wojciechowski whose indispensable help and trust made this book an object in the world.

POETRYCOMICS.ORG

ACKNOWLEDGMENTS